POLYFILLER

BY SARAH CRUTWELL

Copyright © 2018 by Umbrella Poetry

All rights reserved.

This book or any portion thereof
may not be reproduced or used in any manner whatsoever
without the express written permission of the publisher
except for the use of brief quotations in a book review.

Printed in the United Kingdom
Published by: Umbrella Poetry
Author: Sarah Crutwell
Cover Artist: Jess Miller

ISBN: 978-1-5272-3108-5 (paperback)

First Printing, October 2018
First Edition

www.umbrellapoetry.com

Polyamory
is the ability or capacity to love more than one person at a time. Sometimes seen as the practice of, or desire for, intimate relationships with more than one partner, with the knowledge of all partners involved

The Rules.

*If you can't speak honestly about it, without shame,
don't do it.*

*Declare your motives up front – Poly must be out the cage before
you engage.*

*You are in control. If at any point you do not feel it, know you
can get out.*

If it hurts, stop.

*If you see in his eyes that he wants something more
than you want to give, tell him gently.
Leave kindly.*

Don't get attached enough to cry.

Learn. Seek out lessons, listen.

Avoid messy situations – All parties, directly & indirectly involved, must know and consent.

Above all, listen to yourself.

CONTENTS

The Rules
  - - -

The Poly Bird	1
Doodles	2
Poetical Differences	3
Beer Garden Girl Kiss	5
Mechanical	6
Pan Pang	7
Ivory for Elephants	8
Trust Me	10
Saturday Night	11
Bathwater	12
Fucked	14
Daddy Issues	15
Long Story Short	17
Quickie	19
Manic Pixie Dream Girl	20
Needed	22
Thoughts On Accidently Fucking Another Womans Husband	23
Free Spirit	25
Gentle Man	27
PollyFiller	29
Acknowledgements	31

  - - -
The Rules (Revised)

The Poly Bird

Poly wants a cracker, or even just a fucking
crumb of human intimacy and stroked thigh tops
without the complications that come
adding another person, so fully to her life.

Poly preens in cage
finds herself between the lips of men
grows tired of the same tongue tasting her name.

Poly knows when it is *comfortable*,
it is *oh so easy* to fall
meat from her bones
on to the plate of another.

Poly is
        flying,
                falling,
                      flying,
                            falling

Smiling while you do
until the landings
start
to hurt.

Doodles

Always start
etched straight lines
A zig, the odd zag. dots occasionally.
but
as mind and wrist unwind, they relax in to
curls of waves, petals. sometimes, even hearts.

ink spreads page like blood in cheeks

like making sure to meet him in a public place,
then
leaving drinks half drunk,
to fuck in an empty house.

I usually, at least try, to keep straight lines
safe familiar repetition, but my restless
mind wonders, usually south, once I see that
thing, that- *whatever* it is, that makes *this* man
both a lesson and a blessing.

Poetical Differences

Second floor flat, empty-
bar bed, bookcase, desk.
Punch bag nailed to wall.
Three outfits on clothes rail
above two pairs of shoes.

Rest had gone to charity
Said he didn't need *Stuff*

I said
I get it,
I live in storage.

Y'can tell he's always thinking
always working you out.
I notice while I do the same.

I said
I have to see the best in people,
no matter how obvious the evidence
have to believe they are Good.

His boy,
as broken as my girl,
We packaged and serve differently,
observe those who take interest
with suspicion.

He said
I don't, I have to see what people want from me.
People always want something from you.

I asked if this made them *Bad*
and it lingered, floated with the dust
in a room lined with othe words of other men.

We would start, each time,
Me perched on step by door,
Him central, comfortable taking his space.

Talk about living in interesting times,
sitting on opposite sides,
only meeting in middle,
to fuck on the desk.

Once, I curled into him after,
Sweating, shakes, dishevelled,
Hand wrapping his ribs,
he asked what I was doing
I breathed
I forgot, just for a moment,
who we are.

Dressed, rolled for the road, hit it.
Later he wrote about the breeze
and my desperation.

I wrote about the moon.

Beer Garden Girl Kiss

When I said I was sober
    She slipped vodka in my drink

When I said I was single
    She slipped tongue in my mouth

When I said I lived nearby
    She said her boyfriend was inside
    Or I'd lick you dry

Ran her hand under my hem
    Turned with a wink
        Flicking tongue
            Over shoulder
            As she left
        Leaving the door
    Firmly
      Open.

Mechanical

He added, I accepted, he spoke first.
We unfolded ourselves bare and highly sexed
in text and winks. Talked threesomes,
role play, imagined picking out our third–
boy or girl?
Girl.

Fucking another(s) father figure
to rest there till I am ready to be alone again.
We left first drinks, to fuck like we knew each other.
Parts of us seemed to.
We learnt the rest clung naked and sticking
in snatched time of very different lives.

Pan   Pang

I seem to have a knack

of falling for Girls who

like, like Girls but

like, date

Boys

.

Ivory For Elephants

His head was like, three of mine- size wise I mean.
Big enough that I imagine he has trouble buying hats.
Playdough soft, lines laughed deep in older skin,
shiny bald but those eyes, those child wide mischief eyes.

My own head - considerably smaller like coconut and orange.
Tan skin pulled youth thin over stronger than they feel features.

But, I reckon they'd hold the same amount of water.

He told me, his hands in my pockets,
limbs belting him beneath me,
that his job was *'moving water.'*
I imagined him cupping it careful, delicate with those
giants hands. Moving slow steady steps between two lake lungs
loosing not one drip – no cheap trick, just care.

He told me he was raised by strong women.
I could tell by the way he kissed me.
You can taste a man who knows the worth of Woman.

He smiled that smile that folds me in to him, called me *girlfriend*
nine hours after we met.
I scoffed,
pulled back said
I could be anyone- could be evil - might -
hunt elephants for ivory.
He said I couldn't pull the trigger.

Told him I don't do commitment, monogamy, tradition.
He said I couldn't pull the trigger.

I'd become too used to the usual glint in eye, twitch in trousers.
Instead, he breathed slow. Lifted me gently from his lap,
said I *want to see you Monday,*
Tuesday, Wednesday, Thursday, Friday, Saturday
and meet your mam on Sunday.

I laughed, till I remembered how long it had been since a man
tried to make me laugh instead of make me wet,
wondered why I hadn't noticed that til now.
Smiled, *we'll see how Monday goes.*

Still smiling when Monday came
and left
without a call.

I guess he couldn't pull the trigger.

Trust Me

I am skin tired of being told by men,
who I do not know,
that I should trust them
>   to accept that drink
>   to go back to theirs
>   to fly to Skardu

Bone and teeth tired of feeling *Guilty* for not.
Trust despite myself, to be torn skin from bone
by teeth of men who want to own my sex. To have
and to hold.

Saturday Night.

Only one step from feral
dirt cracked feet, wild spun
kicks and half curls on head.
Teeth and nails and open arms
she needs clear exits, clearer
intentions, or she runs.

She made her home
alone in the woods
with a friendly otter,
shared food
and advice on staying alive.

Full moon draws her to village, prowls
bars, bookshops, beaches.
Watches for others, alone,
licking scabs and
watching.

Sniff, circle,
Fuck.

BATHWATER.

smoke spliff sat on pebble bashed bollard. soul music heavy breath in my ears. thinking of you. feeling pulse between crossed thighs. angry crinkled woman gestures fag at me. loudly whispers *fucking blatant as you like, 11am* to the shaking head of a friend. I smile smoked eyes, flick butt to curb saunter sex up concrete steps, to roof terrace flat above *too new* shops. Yours is the garden with picket fence and plastic grass under real trees. the green is a relief from all the grey. prop bag on bench, unzip. mint on tongue, scent on chest. feel excitement slick between my lips open –

push open the door.

light and steam lead my skin to bathroom, where you lay naked, smiling those eyes. cardie slips from shoulders, crumples in pile with the rest of the things we wear to protect ourselves. toes dip into steaming waters, I fold forward on knees. naked. take your chin in my hand, and breath hello into your open mouth, flicking tongue.

the want I feel, swells inside me, seeps out in bathwater. we scoop palms, pour onto each other's shoulders, chests, nipples. bend swan neck down to roll my tongue around your tip.

chill pimpled skin covers full breasts, warmed by wet hands, running rivers down breasts. drips form on pointed nipples. groans echo white tiles. I feel pearls slip from my mind, build inside and flow out of me. diluted by clouded lukewarm water. you stop.

look me in my red raw eyes. hold cum-bathwater hand to my

cheek and kiss me. deep and slow. so slowly.
we breathe between head rolls and kissed necks. slowed to stop, caught in eyes that recognise what each other have seen. don't claim to understand it. don't try to fix it. just accept it. nod slow.

we sat holding on to each other until the water was cold. bubbles melted to reveal shaved pubes in foam life-ring around us. we dried each other using the same radiator warm towel. your chin resting on my head. so close, barely touching skin peels off skin with each heart beat, each moment. hard cock on woman thigh. we curl nakedness around our bodies, laid on blanket floor. pressed my palm against yours. and breathed you. lace woman thighs around your hips, desperate to pull you deep enough to fill me.

Find my lace tangled in sheets
Under cotton clinging to pooled pores
Consent wet on lips
Kissed open waiting thighs so
Easily.
Designed to fit this way.

After Sabrina Mahfouz

Daddy Issues

It's all in the crease of an eye,
I swear, you can tell the ones
filled with worries about daughters finding
the kind of man, they used to be.
It makes them kinder, to me.
Touch softer, thighs decades apart.
I feel safe, they feel wanted. Still,
  it works - til it doesn't.

One kissed my forehead goodnight, habit,
bedtime ritual and I stood at the right height.

Throw back sheets I never expect to sleep in
hop in taxi home. Scribble till I sleep.
Sound of school run wakes him
while I dribble sex and prose into pillow.

When I curl my heart into your man beat chest, I envy
your daughter. envy her mother. How safe they must feel.

A friend told me to fuck my own age, so I tried
but small minded prick, who was not gentle, asked me to call
him daddy. I spat bedsprings, screamed if you want me to call
you father, act like one. Fucked me twice and left sheepish.

So now, I stick to knuckle hairs at least
nose hair to be safe, ear hair to be sure.

Men from generation used to curls creeping knicker elastic,
don't expect pussy shaved sore. Men whose rough
hands rinse tiny tangled heads, laughter bouncing tiles.

Don't get me wrong, I'm not looking to play mummy.
Just for a man, comfortable in his role
teaching his *Girl* to *Woman*.
To know, she deserves a better man
than her father used to be.

Long Story Short

A boy who fucked me once,
badly, in a hotel room he paid for
text me 4 months late to say

long story short,
I'm leaving home
I need to rant at someone
who isn't a friend.
can I stay with you for a while?

long story short
this boy, had laid sure and cocked on pillow
licked lips with expectation and lead my gender
to his crotch because
that's what he watched.

Da Man laying down the law
while woman licks dicks
spits compliments
Big Boy, because
that's what he watched.

Ignoring twisted guts
and instinctive glances to door,
I kneel to attention, heal,
sway hips, stick out tits

because long story short
that's what he wanted.

Tell myself I can show him

Teach him, to enjoy a woman who
enjoys sex with a man who knows
how to appreciate a woman who's tired
of having sex with men who
enjoy using women
like a wank.

That's what *I* wanted

Long story short
he pushed curls flat
to my head
groaned as I gagged
filmed it
because that's what he watched

I tried to show him softness
the tease of finger tips,
being completely at ease
with the body between your knees but

he simply wasn't interested-
    It wasn't what he watched.

Long story short, I stopped trying please men
who were uninterested in trying to please me.

long story short I replied
No.

Quickie

The penis ejaculates at
28mph
You could
be impressed by
that

Or

You could wonder at the
  ability of the vagina
    to take that
      kinda
        shit.

Manic Pixie Dream Girl

She is different to the other girls
or so she's told.

She has
blue hair,
maybe a nose ring.
Maybe she wears clothes three sizes too big
to keep them guessing
or to hide in.

She probably lives in a loft,
a Van, a beach hut
or cupboard.
Blu-Tacs photos of previous selves
pulling faces, poses, people
always laughing, smiling, pleasing
thumbs them to the walls she swears
don't cage her. Mood lit coconut oil
by the mattress on the floor.

She wears her wild between her lips –
something about those lips, the way they move,
are licked, pulled, touched, they way the
camera zooms as she sucks her straw.

Confident leaving the house Friday night with no plans
other than adventure & spare pair of pants.

She is the life he needs to feel alive.
Whoever *He* is this week, month, episode.

He looks at her the way she needs to be looked at sometimes,
when she needs to see her worth in new eyes.

Wraps their angles in her curves, shows them softness
when they need it. Teeth if they take her for granted.

She is the girl who, when asked
Will you run away with me?
replies
Where we going?

Feeds on the temporariness of their need because
being happy alone, has an ugly habit of loneliness.

Needed

Wrap thighs around ego
Soft hands round throat to
take the weight of holding head so high
Sinks in to my soft
Breathes there for while
nursing his pride
in the wounds of my body

Thoughts on accidently fucking another woman's husband

Obviously,
the fucking wasn't accidental,
but I didn't know married part.
Didn't see a wedding ring,
Hadn't learnt to look

Yet.

Didn't feel it slip,
with his conscience between white thighs.

Explains shifting eyes the only time we met outside,
parking round corner,
alibi gym gear,
showering after.

Me scrubbing his back while he soaped questions with
It's complicated.

Too many times life was simpler
before asking questions.

This poem isn't a
how could he fuck me married kinda poem

Or a
How could I be so stupid?

Bunny boiling
Home wrecking
Guilty
kinda poem.

This is a
Does it matter if he's married
kinda poem.

If it is was arranged,
if it was only bonds between families
that pushed them together
only *keeping up appearances*
holding them that way
if there's no love.

This is a
if he can't leave,
if she doesn't hurt
does it depend on the circumstances
kinda poem.

Free Spirit

Hippie pants, meditation swinging from head phones,
beaded bracelets and chunky rings rattling 'round chunky cocks
of strangers, to the tune of freedom

Tokes long drags in young lungs
holds till every part of haze fills her empty
exhaling nothing but sweet breath

Feels the world through bare feet on rough earth
daisy dotted grass, tarmac glittering glass
it's all the same walk of life

Falls in eyes that hold interest in her
steps in their skin, wonders through forgotten footsteps
holds her hand flat pressed against theirs, feels it all

If you can't cope
with feeling it all
leave, coz
she can't help but feel it all
all the fucking time

Told the man who 'saved her'
she couldn't forgive him for breaking her heart
heard the hope leave his body. his mothers last breath

Kick in the gut with all the strength and snarl
of a back hand against a wet cheek

Fists pounding the chest
she curled into
twirling chest hair
Trying
to be free.

The Gentle Man

He keeps himself firmly under his own hand
muted and modest
but when he does talk
it's in lullabies.

He said he's been paranoid in the past.
I said there are parts of me in the past
please don't expect all of me.

The way, he clarifies, checks, reassures,
sooths me with good intentions.
The way, I never needed him to.

There's something in his Emoji's, that just kind of
implies, he'd be truly happy to sleep on the floor-
if that's what I wanted.
Something in his tweed,
that makes me wanna weave
around the ribs of his single bed.
Never leave.

Eleven minutes after we met in person
pressed to person, came together with claws
clinging to something we hadn't had in a long time.
I rode him with hands in my hair,
white knuckles guiding my hips
glanced at what looked like the handle

of an axe,

at the end of the bed.

We stopped.
Panted conversation
confirmed
It was in fact an axe.

But

Something in his mouth
Told me I was safe with this tongue.

Something in the curve of his arm
suggested
more *Woodsman*
than *mad axe murderer.*

This gentle man who loves me wild
And keeps me guessing-
Keeps me smiling.

Who touches me when he doesn't want anything
just to feel I'm still there. still reachable.
sits me silent in lap when ribcage heaves
and hot tears pool on denim knees,
just holds on.

Polyfiller

I think
I used them in a way, not for sex,
though that was had.

Think I used them
as a distraction from myself.
Being tangled head over heels with someone
is a better way to spend a Friday night
than picking self apart.

The *look* is what we are told matters
smooth it down to hide the cracks.
Even with nose pressed to wall,
it would appear I was young, free
YOLO father fucker.
Covered nights sobbing alone in kitchen.

Maybe it's the way we tell the story.

Using each other
VS
Scratching a mutual itch

Hiding from our problems
VS
A moment to rest from it all.

Being sexually empowered
VS
Slagging about

Maybe it's all in the *intention.*

Learning another person, intimately
Good or Bad

Learning myself in the
way I wrap around them
Good or Bad

I hope they learned from me, or at least
remember me smiling.

Acknowledgements

The people in these pages
Thank you
Or fuck you.
You'll know which applies

My Family
I will never know how to thank you enough
For raising me, for all you do...
But I still hope you never read this book!

Flattie & the Buddha Bus
You fucking legends.

The Warrior Writer Women
Who inspire, motivate and empower me.
Your strength, and ability to share weakness
helps me more than you could ever know.

The men
Who taught me
I didn't want anything less
than equal.

Crotchet Lumberjack
You talk me down from panic
Pick me up from stagnant blankets
You love me always,
See me equal
Have my back.

I never knew it could be this good.

The Rules (Revised)

If you can't speak honestly about it, without shame, don't do it.

**I learned to speak honestly by not
hanging my world
on the words of others.**

Declare your motives up front – Poly must be out the cage before you engage.

**Wolves licked their chops,
put thumbs in my mouth, told me
they could see my animal.**

**The Woodsmen told me
they couldn't watch me go to the wolves.**

You are in control. If at any point you do not feel it
know you can get out.

The times you gave to stop them taking.

**The time you didn't leave so as not to hurt his feelings
polite excuses pushed against balcony, entered.**

**You let him fuck you drunk, young, eager
To avoid hurting those doe eyes.**

You are worth more.
If it hurts, stop.

Hurt can be addictive.

If you see in his eyes that he wants something more than you want to give, tell him gently. Leave kindly.

**The look on his face,
when he unexpectedly
dropped round
the day after I'd used
sex with another
as another way
to break myself.**

Don't get attached enough to cry.

**Poly ended
with tears poured into tea cup
On Christmas Day,
wanting the comfort of only him.**

**Monogamy began
Boxing Day after a three hour drive
to his single bed.**

Learn from every inch of it. Seek out lessons and listen.

Keep the lessons, leave the hurt.

Avoid messy situations – All parties, directly and indirectly involved, must know and consent.

**The times you wrapped good intentions
and excuses around their clichés and complications,
are the only times that still itch awake at 3am.**

Above all, listen to yourself

**Darling,
	Keep Listening.**

About The Author

Sarah is a depressed anxious feminist who is mostly found in pajamas or clothes that look suspiciously like pajamas.

A Writer, Spoken Word Poet and creative event organiser from the North East of England, Sarah's work explores the *things we lower our voices to talk about.*

After 7 years in a monogamous relationship, and some time to heal, Sarah decided to dip a bit more than a toe into polyamory. Polyfiller is the result of after date scribbles and 3am questions. Polished, rolled in eco friendly glitter and published.

Enjoy x